WHISPERS
OF THE DEEP

Bittersweet Renewal in a Love Lost
and a Love Found

MORGAN SILAS DONNELLY

**Flotsam and Jetsam Series
Book 2**

Copyright © 2025 by Morgan Silas Donnelly.

All rights reserved. No part of this book may be reproduced or used in any manner without written permission of the copyright owner except for the use of quotations in a book review. For more information, contact: writer@morgansilasdonnelly.com.

ISBN Paperback: 978-1-7382574-5-4
ISBN Electronic: 978-1-7382574-6-1

Publishing Consultant: PRESStinely - PRESStinely.com

This book is a work of fiction. The names, characters, and events in this book are the products of the author's imagination or are used fictitiously. Any similarity to real persons, living or dead, is coincidental and not intended by the author.

Printed in the United States of America.

Morgan Silas Donnelly
Tiny Gnat Publishing

MorganSilasDonnelly.com

Dedication

To those who sneak an early peek at the wrapped gifts that are artfully hidden at the back of someone else's closet.

And to my muse.

Table of Contents

Foreword 9

Introduction 11

Love
and hot tubs and mirrors

I Awoke 14
Sorry 15
Warts And Scars 16
Freely Given 17
The Highest Compliment 18
Complement 19
Truly Yours 21
Alone 23
Airwaves 24
Airwaves
    kindred remix 26
20 fold
    What Would Love Do pt. 2 28
Bonfire Inferno 36
You Know Those Memories 38
You Know Those Memories
    little voice alternate 40
I Remember Well 42
At That Hotel 43
Symbols of Love 45
Got 46
Text Balls Of Emptiness 47
Electricity 49

Gratitude Trick 49
A Match In The Dark 50
Rescue 101 51
Receiving 53
Love Rings Out 54
Messages In The Dark 55
In The Before Times 56
Love Unbound 57
Tidal Wave 58
Girl Tell 60

Connections
and nails and screws

The Most Dangerous Man In The World 62
Replaceable Things 65
The Rhyme of 2023 66
Pave over 67
Shimmer 68
Watermelon 70
Nor You, Nor Me 71
I Kicked A Stick 72
That Path
    friendship remix 77
Bombers
    Hawaii Martin Mars last flight tribute 78
Moth 80
Thumbs Up 81

Life
and addictions and candles

Good Morning World! 84
Sadness 85

Table of Contents

So 86
Knees 86
Leaders 87
Misdirection 87
Ostara Wishes 2023 89
i am what i am 90
Up Messes 91
Staccato 91
One Step 93
Release 94
Spark That 96
Naturally 97
Butterfly Dawn 98
Ok. Ok. Ok. 99
Crashing Ashore 100
Politico 101
Rebirth 102
Dance 103
Out Of Juice 104
Realms 107
Switch? 108
Murky 110
de Detector 112
I Don't Care 113
Untitled 114
Untitled
     alternate beat 115
Things I Think About 117
Letting Go 118
Is? 120
Why 121
i am a candle in the night 122
i am a candle in the night
     alternate 126

Picture Perfect	130
The Sky Is The Sky	132
Cynics	134

Prose
and ribbons and bridges

Coffee Date	138
Crumble	142
the suitcase of mine	144
Message Overlay In 2023	146
Reminded Today	148
Safety	150
Family Array	155
Future Important	157
Here To There	158
Went	160

Ciao Bella

Here At The Rocks	164
Afterword	**167**
Also by Morgan	**169**
Meet Morgan	**171**
The Shipwreck	173
a bonus story	

Foreword

Through my years as a dating and relationship coach I have heard tales of the uncountable ways by which the human spirit is confronted with hard lessons - tales that soap opera writers would find too rich to script.

Morgan's poetry offers a 'beyond the clouds' view of life's journey. With careful discernment, he shares his insights into romance, loneliness, family and ... speed dating (which is, incidentally, how we originally crossed paths – he attended one of my hosted events). His verse is both meaty and whimsical, powerful and graceful, as he crafts poetry to even the most painful moments of human suffering.

As observers of the lives of others, we are able to see more clearly our lives. All the words in this book have been written for you and for me; for our growth, our comfort and the strengthening of the spirit.

Because you value honesty and authenticity, bring Morgan's world into yours. Stay close to him. His writing withholds nothing. It is unfiltered, courageous and exhilarating.

I maintain that suffering is not the worst of all experiences. The worst is, in fact, suffering alone. The more we share, hopes, fears, failures, joys, the more beautiful, the more meaningful, the more magical life becomes.

Aren't we all, as Morgan puts it, 'a little lost, but determined to move forward in life'? I echo this sentiment in my personal mantra: "Life rewards boldness." I believe that setting a goal and taking bold action towards it is never in vain, whether that be looking for support in your journey towards lasting love, sharing your story or simply weathering a trying moment.

Be a witness to the tapestry of experiences exhibited in Morgan's poems. Perhaps they'll feel like your own, as they did for me.

If you've read this far, you haven't yet read enough. Enjoy!

Tamara Del Elis
Dating and Relationship Coach
www.TamaraDelElis.com

Introduction

"These days do not belong to the hewers of wood and drawers of water. These days belong to those who have pure hearts and allow themselves to expand with boundless love. Now the hearts that are ablaze, with eyes that are unfettered, can help those who still live in chains."

I wrote those words down as the events covered in Echoes of the Deep, the companion to this book, wound down. I love the quote for it speaks of bliss, sovereignty, and possibilities beyond which we have known here on Earth.

My words hold love so that you may find in the ashes of their enjoyment, the promise of your life well lived. Where we go from here is up to each of us.

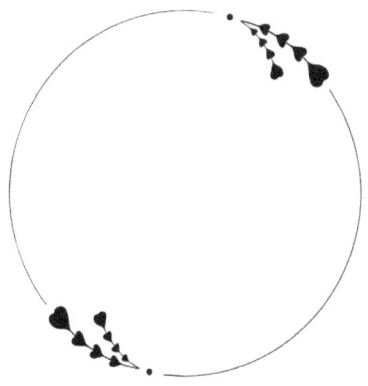

Love

and hot tubs and mirrors

I Awoke

When I awoke this morning
I didn't see your pretty face
                        beside me

Maybe tomorrow I will

~ Love ~

Sorry

I'm sorry for what I said when I was protecting myself

    in unhealthy ways

        and lashed out

Towards someone I love

Warts And Scars

My heart has warts
My heart has scars
My heart has stitches from when I was 5
My heart is misshapen and quite a-
symmetrical

I never knew how beautiful it was
until your love shone on it

~ Love ~

Freely Given

There is a hug I would have more freely given
There is a kiss I wouldn't have parted from
There is a hello I never would have said
There is a goodbye I would have fought harder against

There is a night I wouldn't have slept through
There is a day I would gleefully repeat

For the lovers that left, I extend my hand
For the lovers that will leave, I smile a greeting with a tear in my eye

The Highest Compliment

The highest compliment I can give you

        is

when I think back to you and me

        I smile

~ Love ~

Complement

The highest compliment I know is simply this:

"Being with you showed me where my limitations were."

"Does the formula of your life still support you and those around you?"

~ Love ~

Truly Yours

Dear Love,

This time apart has shown me we need to be together.

Yours truly,

"The divine partner you are calling
is busy working on their shit.
Please try your call again, later."

~ Love ~

Alone

my cup was empty

We met
and Our cups filled up

somehow, someway
my cup emptied

i lashed out

your cup emptied
and
you moved away

i'm working on filling my cup so We can drink again

                    together

Airwaves

airwaves of light
airwaves of love
airwaves of tears
airwaves of joy

I have tears in my eyes
reading notes
reading confidences
reading observances
reading of a love that crumbled

airwaves of love

I am watching a sci-fi show
letters for home
letters for loved ones
letters of longing
across time and space
of the fictional kind

airwaves of light

I have tears on my cheeks
knowing that I have but to reach out
once more, and feel love's true kiss
in the song of my heart

airwaves of joy

~ Love ~

I am drinking a bitter draught
a potion
made bitter by the saline
tracks of a heart break that is salient

airwaves of tears

Airwaves
kindred remix

airwaves of light
airwaves of love
airwaves of tears
airwaves of joy

I have tears in my eyes
reading notes
reading confidences
reading observances
reading of love's bind

airwaves of love

I am watching a sci-fi show
letters for home
letters for loved ones
letters of longing
across time and space
of the fictional kind

airwaves of light

I have tears on my cheeks
knowing that I have but to reach out
once more, and feel love's true kiss
in the song of hearts entwined
airwaves of joy

~ Love ~

I am drinking a potion
a bitter draught
made ever more bitter by the saline
tracks of a heart break malign

airwaves of tears

20 fold
What Would Love Do pt. 2

The mirrors in their hall
The masquerade ball
All dancers and prancers
reflected
20 fold

The woman goes in
Such a lovely dress
Bows and lace
in cold blues
She never gave a thought
to how her heart was a mess

The man is there
He has always been there
searching and searching
All his reflections
just leave him lurching
He doesn't have time
to do some heart searching

He beds for the night
No stars in the sky
just himself
20 fold

He came into this place

~ Love ~

to hide from the pain
that is his deep inside
Not realizing his fate
the mirrors reflect all
hate
20 fold

She wonders and wanders
at the sight of herself
delight
20 fold

She came into this place
for true love's kiss
To seek that which
they say is bliss
The mirrors give back
longing
20 fold

He awakens to a noise
A floorboard's creak
"How strange. There is no one
else here!"
just me
20 fold

She gasps at the noise
her slippers have made
"This board is loose.
No ghosts here, no love, no bliss!
Oh silly girl, oh silly goose!
Hum that tune to keep the frights away."

Whispers of the Deep

A melody reaches him
He opens one eye
"Tricks of the mind.
No radio, no orchestra, no chanteuse.
Be strong. Get a grip.
Your mind is not loose."

He closes his eye
and searches for slumber
She reaches inside
and remembers the number
A tune she recalls
from her childhood tumbles
echoed
20 fold

"Oh dear lass
Dry the tears
What you fear
will soon pass
Sniffles and snorts
make a face red
There there child
take a look at your dread
The occasional tumble
makes one humble
There, there child
It doesn't look bad
Living life doesn't have to be sad"

He opens his eyes
and gets up to yell
"I know who you are!
My mind has splintered!

~ Love ~

My mind has cracked!
You are not of this world!
I am here!
All alone!
Stop leering, get out of my head!!
My heart, it is bled!
My passion, it fled!
My tears, so dry!
I am a shell
of a man who can not even try!
You infernal mirrors!!"
seething
20 fold

A deep voice without
beyond her safe place
"Who is there?
Is it me?
My heart is that you?
A voice not mine!
Heart, can you project
a spectre of sorts?
Is that what you do?"
The puppets of her heart
mumble
20 fold

For the first time
he saw such a light
The mirrors were not cracked
The mirrors still reflected
They were, in fact, intact
His body reacted
Tears to protect

Whispers of the Deep

his eyes that had failed
He moved to the light
He moved towards her
The other who wailed
sobbing
20 fold

Through glass and wood
his body moved
Not knowing how
but he did what he could

There she was
that lady in blue
She glowed like a candle
and to his sight true

She lifted her eyes
to see a man all in white
who glowed quite darkly
like a creek in pale night

She looked like a dream
He looked like fantasy
They moved towards each other
They touched
A trap it did seem

A spark, a thunder clap
The room went white
They blink, in a daze
Each seeing the other
in a brand new light

~ Love ~

They blinked again, still dazed
by the loud silent knowing
that they had been found
ecstatic
20 fold

They touch once again
and feel the connection

But wait! What is this?
Something is wrong!

They fall to their knees
struggling for breath
They spied around
to find two hearts on ground

She looked quite ashen
He reaches a heart
that he passes to her
She takes it well in
to gulp air with passion

He falls back, now unsteady
and weak
She lifts the lone heart
Well braced
she presses and squeezes
This heart of his, replaced

He gasps the air and sees his love
Not like she was
He has longing
He has wanting

Whispers of the Deep

She has hate
She has pain

He too has changed
Having lost his fury
He is softer
Not in a hurry
gentler
20 fold

"I feel strange my love!"

"I feel strange too!"
Is this a trick?
Is this a treat?
I know you
But I sense
you were far more down beat
In unison they say
"Perfect timing!"
20 fold

"This change is not me.
The mirrors bore witness
to my defeats.
This change is you!
For now your heart beats
in place of my own!"

"Oh! Let's change
Let's exchange
Let's remove the wrong one!"

~ Love ~

"No, hold on, it feels better.
I feel more me.
I feel more complete.
Let's not be undone."

"Yes, I feel
like never before.
Like heroes true
in the stories of lore."

Do we switch?
Do we change?
How is this?

I have yours
and you have mine
and we seem tied
as if by a line

Not yet as flesh
Not yet as bone
but deep, deep inside
our hearts beat true
Not alone
20 fold

Dance after dance
will love have clout
Each for the other
until time runs out
20 fold

Bonfire Inferno

Love can be the instant inferno, the sentence finishing, the unspoken silence, the outrageous laughter, the raging heat of a soul to soul connection when two lovers collide.

Love can also be the spark that lights the smokey, sputtering flame that one gingerly adds small, small kindling to with the deep, deep hope to have it grow in time to a large, large fire than ever was before.

~ Love ~

"The fuel you add to love is the thing indeed -- not too much,
not too little, not too fast, not too slow."

You Know Those Memories

That certain cafe.
That incredible view.
The smells that intoxicate.
The sounds that come.
crashing in
crashing in
crashing in

That moment of a deep breath to really feel like you are alive.
The next, a voice sounds off behind you speaking
nothing mean, nothing nasty, nothing at all really.

Just the same voice as your someone.
That same someone you are fighting with
right now.
That same someone you are mad at
right now.

You hear their voice, their inflections, their word salad.

You turn around, slowly, unbelieving in the chances it could
be them out here in the wilderness.
In the flesh.
A chance to discuss, a chance to reconnect.

You scan the crowd, you scan the din, you scan the dim.

You find the voice, you see the face

but it is not them.

~ Love ~

You turn back, more slowly this time.
The room seems larger than it did a moment ago.
You take your time, you blink the tears.
You grab the table to steady yourself.

Before picking at your food once more.
This time more slowly than ever before.

That certain cage.
That certain look.
That certain moment of dread.
crashing in
crashing in
crashing in

You Know Those Memories
little voice alternate

that certain cafe
that incredible view
the smells that intoxicate
the sounds that come
crashing in
crashing in
crashing in

that moment of a deep breath to really feel like you are alive

the next, a voice sounds off behind you
nothing mean, nothing nasty, nothing at all really

just a similar voice
just a disagreement
just not speaking to each other right now

their voice you think you hear
their inflections
their word salad

you turn around, slowly, unbelieving in the chances it could be them
in the flesh

you scan the crowd
you scan the din
you scan the dim

~ Love ~

you find the voice, you see the face

but it is NOT them

you turn back, more slowly this time
the room seems larger than it did a moment ago
you take your time
you blink the tears
you grab the table to steady yourself

before picking at your food once more
this time more slowly than before

that certain cage
that certain look
that certain moment of dread
crashing in
crashing in
crashing in

I Remember Well

No, I don't remember the name of your dog that died when you were 5
No, I don't remember your birthday
No, I don't remember the way you like your coffee

What I remember is a woman I could talk to
What I remember is a woman who squeezed my hand when I reached for hers
What I remember is joy
What I remember is laughter
What I remember is connection

When I look at the ashes of what we had together

                I remember

~ Love ~

At That Hotel

This hotel has a soaker tub
I haven't been in one since,
since .... since ....

The kind with no jets
The kind I like
The kind you put up with
but didn't prefer

It's got a back rest for you
It's got a back rest for me
I put my feet up
where your kidneys would be

I remember how you looked
when you were in a tub
Your skin kinda glistening
from the steam of it all
Sometimes you would smile
an awkward smile
Sometimes you would not
be awkward at all

Just pure guitar rifts
and champagne popping
at that hotel

"Fear makes us do silly things.
Pain allows us to do troubling things.
Love creates magnificent things."

~ Love ~

Symbols of Love

I sit here with two symbols on my table
Two symbols of loves
past and done
They sit side by side
                              in my vision
                  and in my heart
        and in my brain

Two symbols that never met until the other night
They greeted each other cooly and acceptably
The opposite of how they sit in my brain

Two symbols that have aged and sagged
in the short time they have had each other
The opposite of how they sit in my heart

Two symbols that glow and shine
with the promise of forever and promises kept
The opposite of how the women sit in my vision

Got

Got rockstar parking today.

Dreamt of the love of my life caressing me so.

I asked the Universe for the more of this good stuff. I like the feeling of bliss and the ease it comes with.

I also asked the Universe for an equal measure of the not-so-good stuff. I learn and grow with its bitter draught.

I am ready for my cup to be filled, I am thirsty in this desert life.

"I stopped looking for you."

~ Love ~

Text Balls Of Emptiness

"It's her birthday today, again
this year."

"Can you say something to make
me feel better and not text her?"

"I don't want to get silence in
return again this year."

"I can only think of one."

"You are stronger than you
know."

"Missing her is ok."

"Texting her is not."

It is time for Love to stop whispering.

~ Love ~

Electricity

I allow myself

to magnetize a heart

         to me

that will electrify

         me

Gratitude Trick

It's easy to be grateful for the happy.
The trick is to be grateful for the pain too
.. eventually.

A Match In The Dark

You once lit a match in the dark for me

I was alone
I was afraid
I was cold

I would light a bonfire in your heart
so that you can find your way home

~ Love ~

Rescue 101

I don't need to rescue you
      ... you have rescued yourself

      my light shows the path ahead ...
You don't need to rescue me

"The Dance of Coupling is beautiful to behold but the Symphony that accompanies Lovers has octaves beyond the scales of knowing."

~ Love ~

Receiving

I would love to spend many
many

.

.

many nights

giving and receiving
Sweet Pleasure with you

I am very good to my Woman

.

.

as I suspect you are very good to
your Man

Love Rings Out

Love rings out in clear black night
A bell without sound
A fire without heat
A jury without sight

Love rings out in clear dewy dawn
A blue bird sings
A kettle whistles
The village comes alive
A doe nuzzles her fawn

Love rings out in clear bright day
Workers yell instructions
Coffee is poured
Dogs go for walks
Recess arrives, and children play

Love rings out across the miles
Across the waves
Across the chasms
To the stars and to the heavens
when sweet memories bubble up
and smiles erupt
on the two who share knowing
of how sweet love can be

~ Love ~

Messages In The Dark

Messages in the dark can be
screams
Messages in the dark can be
bone chilling silence in your nightmare dreams

Messages in the dark can be
flashlight tag
Messages in the dark can be
a firefly's zig zag

Messages in the dark can be
the pulling up of covers
Messages in the dark can be
the memory of lovers

Messages in the dark can be
the loosening of a tie
Messages in the dark can be
a long slow sigh

Messages in the dark can be
your love light shining

Your love light shining can be
a message in the dark

In The Before Times

Before the Word spoken

was Love unfettered.

Do not You understand

    what Love can do?

"Them: 'You are not this or that!'
Me: 'Close your eyes and look to my heart.
You will see that indeed, this or that is there,
alive and well.'"

~ Love ~

Love Unbound

Love unbound is a dangerous thing
fears will melt + worlds created
when a heart is unwound

The river's dam holds back
tears, laughter, and kisses
the wise man knows safety is a damn

Seasons change and lovers cry
love is strange + unbound
to a heart that has
      u n w o u n d

Whispers of the Deep

Tidal Wave

I saw our love as a tidal wave.
Immense!!
Powerful!!
Frightening!!
Slightly misbehaved!!

This thing of beauty.
This thing of terror.
It came towards me.
Rushing!
Deafening!
Immovable!

And it touched me not!
My clothes were dry.
My hair unruffled.
My shoes not soggy.

It passed
as a cloud on a sunny day,
a wisp in the firmament,
a ballon of cotton

I looked on the shore
afterwards
to find pretty rocks
to find new shells
to see what had come
with the rage of all nature

~ Love ~

and what did i find?
some slime!
intrigued ...
investigate ...
research ...
comprehend ...

it was me
the me that was not
the me that was low
the me that was false

and then i knew
that the wave of our love
touched
striped
healed
but only to show
the beauty inside

Girl Tell

Girl, let me tell you I ain't perfect
I still got some bandages on my heart
that ain't been ripped off yet
but my scars

<<the nasty ones>>

they done heal up

Connections

and nails and screws

The Most Dangerous Man In The World

I am the most dangerous man in the world. I help little old ladies cross the street.

I am the most dangerous man in the world. I say hello to perfect strangers.

I am the most dangerous man in the world. I let others go ahead in line ups.

I am the most dangerous man in the world. I laugh with my friends. I cry with my friends.

I am the most dangerous man in the world. I have forgiven my lovers who crushed me.

I am the most dangerous man in the world. I have forgiven myself for being crushed.

I am the most dangerous man in the world. I have boundaries.

I am the most dangerous man in the world for I know that a woman's heart is stronger than a man's muscles.

I am the most dangerous man in the world even though I need a stepladder to reach the good china plates.

I am the most dangerous man in the world as I have seen a face of God.

~ Connections ~

I am the most dangerous man in the world for I remember who I truly am.

I am the most dangerous man in the world for I can see your soul as plain as day and the pain it reeks and the numbness you seek.

I am the most dangerous man in the world as you can plainly see. Games and hidden agendas are for charlatans and fools.

I am the most dangerous man in the world, for I have dropped my blood soaked sword and fallen to my knees to weep for those I conquered.

This most dangerous man in the world has unchained his heart. It was brittle and small and cold and lifeless. It was to be trifled with, manipulated and then cast aside.

The most dangerous man yelled at the wind to stop blowing. It blew harder.

The most dangerous man in the world stopped yelling. The wind died down.

"Job #1:
Love Humanity"

~ Connections ~

Replaceable Things

Me: "There are millions of missing and murdered women and girls worldwide every year."

Them: "meh...."

Me: ...

Me: "There is a bank robbery down the street!"

Them: "Grab your guns boys! We are rolling everything we got!! They took something that is replaceable!!"

The Rhyme of 2023

I came out of my shell
and found life wasn't hell
People were people
just dealing with stuff
Most are quite nice
if you give them no guff
The tables had turned
as I have learned
The damage inside
is the damage outside
Repair, repair
do not fall to despair
The joy is in merging
the upper and lower
The harmony inside
is the harmony outside
and knowing what is true
the nail from the screw

~ Connections ~

Pave over

Pave over the unmarked grave.

Mask those who are healthy.

Sterilize those who question their sexuality.

Yolk the beast of burden.

Market problems, not solutions.

Restrict travel to those who can afford private jets.

Encourage more taxpayers to be born.

Stamp out gentleness and tenderness at a young age, so they never become dreamers, poets or dancers.

Shimmer

I am not sure how much you understand how much I care about you.
I am not sure how much you understand
how much my soul shimmers when it comes near you.

I can use pretty words.
I can give you banquets and bouquets of roses.
I can give you a child.
Perhaps a fantastic book would be yours
if I could help you understand.

The shimmer I feel is as a pond
on a crystal clear day.
Sun shining,
rippling on the water.
The birds singing
the fish swimming
and the turtles enjoying themselves.

The shimmer I feel is not unique.
The shimmer I feel has been felt before
but with you the colour is unique.

The shimmer itself happens every time.

Everyone
everywhere has a shimmer.
The shimmer I have with you is very comfortable
and irritating
and complacent.

~ Connections ~

It helps me understand the reflection I am to you.

The shimmer.

Watermelon

That day …

That girl …

Wore a unique fragrance of watermelon.

Why did she have to pick watermelon?

That day will live with me a long time.

Of all the days …

Of all the things …

Of all the perfumes …

Watermelon.

~ Connections ~

Nor You, Nor Me

I hear the angels sing
I see the fairies dancing
I feel the roar of the dragons
No child, I am not ordinary
And neither are you

I Kicked A Stick

I kicked a stick
There was no
sage to my rage

It made a noise
I looked with new eyes
On the ground
it did rebound

Over to it I went
to grab it's slab
It tingled and mingled
with the joy of my tears

This stick was mine
Long journey ahead

It had a heft
that pulled me left

Over hills
Over dales
Adventures ahead!
Mind filled with tales
of I and my stick

The trail went to mud
My heart beat faster
as memories flood
of times with a thud

~ Connections ~

My stick was there
to keep me straight
I was upright
Intact was my freight

For I have baggage
far too heavy for me
I keep old memories
in a sack on my back
My stick let me carry them
longer than ever

My stick is my friend
My stick is my shield
Together we go
until the end

A bump, a lump
The road was quite rocky
A snap, a nap
and I woke in a bad

My ankle was bloated
My ankle was bruised
To God I prayed
My body abused

My teeth did grind
as I fought to stand
on the path so rocky
My tears they laughed
at my crafted manhood

Whispers of the Deep

Up I stood
My stick and I
but my bag!
On the ground it did lie

My hopes!
My dreams!
To bend was a fright
I screamed at the sight
of a goal
so near
            so far
                      so dear

I twisted and turned
My stick to assist
But that bag
to my reach
did resist

I gasped and muttered
ungoddess words

I had a choice
I had a dilemma
My memories of old
or my new found oedema

One or t'other
Decide their fate
No one around
No one to blame
My discord did elate

~ Connections ~

One or t'other
will stay or go
Which was best?
Who could know!

I hobbled with my friend
on a rock strewn path
Together now
until the end

"Blow on the clouds like so many candles on a birthday cake."

~ Connections ~

That Path

friendship remix

I have done terrible good things
I have done beautiful bad things
I have broken bones and had mine broken too

There is a love inside
a soft, gentle voice
I hardly hear it
when the ego wind blows

The voice whispers
"forgive, forgive"
"unite, unite"
"rejoice, rejoice"

and still I plod the well worn path
of he said, she said
in my soft, soft brain
The track quite entrenched
of my beliefs I defend
and defend
and defend again
and the hurt that grows

Each time I walk again
that well worn path

Bombers
Hawaii Martin Mars last flight tribute

There are bombers
that rage
There are bombers
that kill
There are bombers
that believe they are sage

There are Bombers
that play
There are bombers
that drink
There are bombers
that believe they have a say

But the bomber I love
is red and white
She floats like a swan
and roars like a lion
and flies like a leaf

She was a war bird
but her master won
before she was flamed

I knew her best
for her courage and bravery
at putting out fires
in home land of mine

~ Connections ~

It was the test of time she stood
and in my heart
I knew she would always win battles
of heat and smoke

I love her so much
for the hope that she gave me
the little boy
that his home would stand free

Moth

My moth floats around
Flying here, flying there
just out beyond the firelight

I invite her in
She skitters here, she skitters there
just out beyond the campfire heat

She catches my gaze
She dances here, she dances there
Her beauty caught in the firelight
as our hearts connect

For a moment,
I am her and she is me
Soaring high, soaring low
moving along to the dance of life

Connect, connect

Disconnect, disconnect
as she heads to the flame

~ Connections ~

Thumbs Up

Yesterday, I was driving on the highway. I came up on a truck towing a really cool vehicle behind it.
As I passed him, the driver looked over and I gave him the thumbs up sign.

This morning, it occurs to me to ask how many of us are giving the thumbs up to other people on this miraculous journey of life? Are you asking each other "hey man, that is a really cool ride. What do you love best about it?" or "wow lady, I love that you kept this retro vehicle mostly factory with a couple really amazing personal touches. That's so great!"

Now, of course, in the greater scheme, I am not talking about automobiles, but rather how many of us are encouraging each other to live life genuinely -- authentically -- firmly heart centred and soul acknowledging? Are you following someone else's dreams ("be a doctor when you grow up", "artists starve!", "activists are scum" etc etc etc)

Changing gears, what is it about the comparison game that humans can so easily slip into? "Oh, that person over there can walk and chew bubblegum at the same time. I always choke when I try that. I am a loser...." NO! You are not a loser, you have many gifts that shine brightly --- the problem is that they come so naturally to you, that they don't come up on your radar of knowing and trusting.

Whoever you are, you are enough. And I joyfully give you a thumbs up!

Life

and addictions and candles

Whispers of the Deep

Good Morning World!

It's a beautiful day ...

...player 1 ready...
...program commencing...
...simulation #19477...
...begin...

~ Life ~

Sadness

Sadness is a wonderful emotion, but you don't need to serve it tea and crumpets by your fireplace.

So

So,

this time are you going to run?

or

will you stand in your power that is yours alone?

Knees

Fear never solved anything ....
So why do we hit our knees so quickly
when it approaches?

~ Life ~

Leaders

Leaders lead from the front lines

Cowards cower from a back office

Terrorists terrorize behind keyboards

Misdirection

Which way to go?

Go where the Light is.

Or where it isn't.

"Terrified means you're going to kick ass."

~ Life ~

Ostara Wishes 2023

For me, I find it's a step by step, by step backwards, by step forwards kinda journey lately.

The programming and overlays of discordant belief systems can be challenging to overcome -- no doubt.

I AM finding the more I go quiet and still, I listen to my heart and it sings of

/ new /
/ different /
/ improved /

options for me to step lightly on the path of life.

I wish you a delightful path this Ostara / Equinox.

Whispers of the Deep

i am what i am

I am human
I am spirit
I am in love
I am in hate
I am of the light
I am of the dark
I am whole
and I am broken
I am human
I am animal
I am mineral
I am flesh
and I am blood
I am heterosexual
I am homosexual
I am omnisexual
I am genderless
I am masculine
I am feminine
I am of the mind
I am of the heart
I am of the soul
I am all that is
All that will be
and all that was

It is so, so amazing to be here on this planet like I am

~ Life ~

Up Messes

I'd rather be messed up at midnight by coffee than messed up at midnight on drugs.

Staccato

flow and go /
stop and stammer /
dream and fly /

    move and live

"Do what we could not do."

– your ancestors

~ Life ~

One Step

What used to take one step
now takes many.

It will take one step again.

- excerpt from the parable "Titan's Journey"

Release

The worm can die
in the cocoon
The butterfly can
emerge when the time is nigh
The wait can be long
with nothing to see

Oh don't you know dear soul
what is happening unseen?

Why are you afraid butterfly?
You only have to choose to break the veil
and fly free of your bonds
Why are you afraid worm?
in the goo and the muck
that is transforming you
Is there a need to worry?
Is there a need to fret?
Can you trust?
Do you need a vision
of the beauty inside?
No, not now
Now there is goo
and an unsettled feeling

Soon

when you release that which was
for that which is coming

~ Life ~

A new life to lead
A new life to cherish
The old life is gone

"You remember it going horribly, horribly wrong. What if you remember it going horribly right?"

Spark That

If you truly believe you can't affect a room

        raise it up and
Spark your lighter

        slowly
            wave it
                over
            your
      head
            as you
      slowly
            sway

~ Life ~

Naturally

The universe is benevolent

The problem is we have been demoralized
beaten down and branded much

so our natural nature is to
      naturally ask very deficient
           asks

Butterfly Dawn

I understand the butterfly in the chrysalis'
desire to break free
I can whisper struggle and strife
are the key

The blood will flow to make you strong
Move your wings against the case

The butterfly won't understand me
in its casing strong
It will need to feel the instinct
if it wants to be distinct

I see the beauty from afar
as it twirls
as it stirs
in a comfort that is no longer the case

The long night falls
I fall asleep
and in the morning dew draped
I see my friend has escaped
while I sat watch for the new Dawn

~ Life ~

Ok. Ok. Ok.

I vacuumed the whole house today...

Ok, I found the vacuum and put it in the hallway so I would trip over it until I was ready to vacuum the whole house...

Ok, ok. What actually happened was I remembered I have a vacuum. I have no idea where it is though...

Ok, ok, ok. I really have no idea if I own a vacuum.

and the house isn't even that dirty anyway...

"Hope is a designer drug."

Crashing Ashore

Light the Match
That lights the Light House
That shines a Light
That saves the Ship
From crashing Ashore

~ Life ~

Político

I am not against politics.

I am against politics that excludes the Heart in decisions.

Rebirth

Break free
Live free
Die free
Reborn

~ Life ~

Dance

Dance with the Light
Dance with the Dark
Dance with your Heart
Dance with God

Out Of Juice

The clock on the wall
it tells one time
10:52
24/7/365
One day
it ran out of juice

Our love is a note
you sealed with a kiss
it sits on a shelf
my voicemail is empty
24/7/365
One day
it ran out of juice

My car is in park
my car does not go
24/7/365
One day
it ran out of juice

Summer was hot
sweet memories made
in a time that has been
24/7/365
One day
it ran out of juice

My body it now lays
in a hole damp and dark

~ Life ~

24/7/365
One day
it ran out of juice

To live and to breathe
to rejoice and to feel
this life is worth living
24/7/365
Day by day
when you fill it with juice

"Them: do you believe in all that stuff?"
"Me: we are all that stuff and more!"

~ Life ~

Realms

The realm of defeat
Ain't nothing but a playground teaching you
how to lay a foundation for success.

Switch?

Is love a switch?
You loved me sweet
You loved me tender
You called me your best friend
Now you don't call at all

Did a switch get flipped?
How can emotions be on
such a roller coaster ride?

I feed the birds big handfuls of peanuts
Not the screaming, demanding birds
but the smaller, shy birds that sing
I shoo away the bully birds
to feed my song birds

Do I have a switch inside for
what birds are good
and
what birds are bad?

One moment there is no life
inside a woman
Then the next she is a mummy
Then the next that little life is
gone
and now she is a mummy to
one-that-is-gone

~ Life ~

Did a switch get flipped?
How is life here
then is not-here
The joy, the heartache,
the laughter and the smiles and the tears
all a memory now

I want a switch
on the memories too
so I don't have to hurt
so I don't have to remember
the pain
the promise
the coulda beens

"Because sweet sister, you are important too."

Murky

In the murky light of the early morning kitchen
I saw a leaf under the counter

A leaf that had blown in from the door
being opened yesterday for the
fixers to come and fix what they fix

I chose not to ignore it, not to sweep it under
even more out of sight

I grabbed support
I held on to the counter top

I bent down
I bent down
I reached out
I reached out

'til my hand closed upon the leaf
a soft leaf
a very soft leaf
a squishy soft leaf

...it was not a leaf...

My hand recoiled
as if on it's own

flight or fight
or stand your ground

~ Life ~

fight or flight
or stand your ground

stand your ground
or flight or fight

a heart beat
a breath
a blink
a stare
comprehension stirring

Oh, it is but a 'bunny!
untethered by the fixers
disturbing the dust that lies all around
this kitchen of mine

Laughing, I bend yet again
to pick up the thing
that was mine all along

How often we recoil
from a thing that is fair

Whispers of the Deep

de Detector

You are getting good at detecting bullshit

because you are getting comfortable with recognizing

                                          your own brand of it

~ Life ~

I Don't Care

I don't care what politician you voted for
I don't care how much money is in your bank account
I don't care what car you drive
I don't care if you are carnivore or vegan

I do care that you believe

                you are worthy
of
                love and great things

Untitled

I walked on a twilit path
muddy, from the storm that passed

I found a maple leaf
wet and abandoned from it's maple
tossed by the wind to the safety of a pine

Where it hung proud but upside down
in the glory of its moist new found freedom
I looked up up up at the tall tall pine
and moved to pluck the leaf from its perch
It hung as it were
rightside downside

It stayed proud and true
Not bending to the rain's mensurations of it's worth
I twirled it
I twirled it again
It fell apart
The flesh, now crumpled and disheveled
was quite apart from the stem

~ Life ~

Untitled

alternate beat

I walked on a twilight lit path
Muddy, from the storm that passed
A falling
                              leaf
Another falling
                              leaf

Seasons are changing
<< as are the clocks >>
the air is   cool

Winter is coming
but the Spring will be
                        glorious

The water drips down
from high above
caught no more
in the glory of a
                        tree

Humans, oh they make noise,
but so does the forest
if one but listens

"Trust the divine, trust your coffee machine, trust your purpose, trust the printer will work."

~ Life ~

Things I Think About

If a mother takes her love away, will a child still grow?
If a mother smoothers the child with love, will the child still grow?

Which way does the wind blow and why does it never seem to go "up"?
Can the wind blow hard enough to flatten you?

If your belief is strong enough, can you create a world?
If your belief is weak, how do you stand on the world another has created?

If your eye offends you pluck it out.
If your neighbour's eye offends you, can you pluck it out as well?

When the dust has settled, and the embers are low,
will you sit at the fireplace and be my friend?

Letting Go

Letting go of the past so that the future can arrive in style

~ Life ~

"Due to galactic copyright laws, armed conflict in your jurisdiction is not allowed."

Is?

Is your niceness to others

                killing

your kindness to you

~ Life ~

why

If it is fluid and changeable,
why are you attached to

                it?

i am a candle in the night

i am but a candle
in the wild, wide, wylde night
a shadow over there
a noise over there
to keep me company

scary, frightening
dim my light
go unnoticed
go undetected

i am but a candle
a woman approaches
she, the she without light,
sees my light
dim as it is
she comes closer
cautiously
carefully
contritely

i know she is there

she has no candle
she has no light
she asks if i will go with her
for this place is frightful
and there is much dark
we hear a howl at that moment
off

~ Life ~

in the distant
dark
black as night
deep as the ocean
heavy as a rock

i say yes
for i have no legs to move about
and she has no light to show the path

another shadow moves
another howl renders the night
she quickly grabs me
and i light up bright

the path is there
just a little away

the stones are smooth
and sparkle in my pale light

she moves with a purpose
she moves with a plan
though i know not what that is

we come to a man
he, the he who is silent and still,
he has a new candle and much fear in his eyes
they sparkle and glow
at the sight of the girl

words are exchanged
a gentle touch

Whispers of the Deep

my gift is my spark
and gladly i give
to the man who knows candles naught

she, the she who can burn,
glows bright without fear
i know her, of sorts,
we came from the same place
though i am older

she, the she holding me,
bids us walk for awhile
i welcome the company
of the candle i once knew
and the humans who are new

we come to more humans
in ones and twos
they all have candles
but no sparks of their own

she, the she who is lit,
gives of herself
as i gave of me

me, the i of me,
gives of himself
as it delights me
to see the path sparkle
of the road up ahead

candles are like that
we can be dim

~ Life ~

we can be extinguished

but we roar loudest
when we light up the dark night

i am a candle in the night
alternate

i am but a candle
in the wild, wide, wylde night
a shadow over there
a noise over there
to keep me company

scary, frightening
dim my light
be protected
go unnoticed
go undetected

i am but a candle
a woman approaches
she sees my light
dim as it is
she comes closer
cautiously
carefully
contritely

i know she is there
i know she is fair
she has no candle
she has no light

she asks if i will go with her
for this place is frightful

~ Life ~

and there is much dark
she gives a smile
so light and delightful

we hear a howl at that moment off in the distant dark
it stirs emotion black as night
deep as the ocean
heavy as a rock

i say yes
for i have no legs to move about
and she has no light to scout
we would be a pair
much stronger than alone

another shadow moves
another howl renders the night
she quickly grabs me
and i turn up the dimmer
to burn bright

the path is there
just a little away
she moves us both
in a style of ballet

the stones are smooth
and sparkle in my pale light

she moves with a purpose
she moves with a plan
she sings of habeas corpus
though i know not what that is

Whispers of the Deep

we come to a man
who is silent and still
he has a candle and much fear in his eyes
they sparkle and twirl
at the sight of the girl

words are exchanged
a gentle touch
my gift is my spark
and gladly i give

his candle glows bright
she glows without fear
i know her, of sorts,
we came from the same place
she rejoices in tear

she, the she holding me,
bids us walk for awhile
i welcome the company
of the candle i once knew
and the humans who are new

we come to more humans
in ones and twos
they all have candles
but no matches to handle

she, the she who is lit,
gives of herself
as i gave of me

~ Life ~

me, the i of me,
gives of himself
as it delights me
to see the path sparkle
on the road up ahead

candles are like that
we can be dim
we can be extinguished

but we roar loudest
when we light up the dark night

Picture Perfect

I have a picture of a beautiful girl on my phone. Yes, she has always been beautiful. But this day, the day of the photo, she did her nails, she did her hair, she spent extra time getting her makeup on. She picked out a nice dress that had been at the back of her closet.

She put aside, for a little while, all the must-do's that a mother must do. She focused on herself and the evening ahead. Selfish? Hmmm, let's call it self-care instead.

I don't know what she was doing, or where she was going. But I do know it would be with her husband. Oh yeah, she's married to another man.

I took off my phone screen a picture of a beautiful sunset and exchanged it with a picture of the face of this beautiful woman instead.

I have the photo of another's man wife on my phone, for a little while anyway. Creepy? Perverse? Hmmmm, let's call it self-care instead.

I put beautiful pictures on my phone's wallpaper all the time. Sunsets, puppies, interesting architecture -- the list goes on. I love bringing the feeling of that wonderful sunset, that playful pup, that magnificent building into my being-ness as I briefly look at it before continuing my day. I want more sunsets in my life, I want more puppies in my life, I want more moments of awe in my life so I put them in front of me.

~ Life ~

The woman? She's just a woman. She's just a beggar. She's just a thief. She's a no-one and she's a goddess, all in one package. Is she perfect? Is she polished? Hmmm, let's call her practiced at self-care.

I don't know her. Not in person. Maybe never will. Maybe she is wearing sloppy pants, with her hair in a sloppy bun now, in this right fair now. Don't know, don't care.

Her beauty, her light, her magnificent feminine charm is what I would like more in my life. Someone beside me, beautiful and bold, warm and tender. Not a ball, not a chain, but a partner in love and a partner in joy. I can bring the rest, I'm a man of the world. But that feminine charm she displays with ease? That is what is missing as I drive down the road.

So if you please, I will continue to put sunsets, puppies, buildings and women on my phone as I please. Those are my needs. My heart swells thinking of them. I know how to self-care.

My steps are lighter when they are walked with love.

The Sky Is The Sky

I took a deep breath
I got real high

I lost focus on my troubles
and the sky came into view

I found people caring about,
caring about things
not caring about people

They cared about the day
and they cared about the night
All the things that the sky cares not
for the sky is the sky
whether is black
or is blue
the sky is the sky

For the sky is the sky
with clouds of fluff
or filled with lightning
the sky is the sky

The child reaches out
to the sky upon sky
A pilot reaches up
a little bit higher

For the sky is the sky
filled with longing

~ Life ~

filled with wonder
filled with dreams
filled with songs
the sky is the sky

Cynics

Cynics never build anything
Dreamers never wake up
Romantics never see
Workaholics never relax
Neurotics never find stability
Adventurers never stay home
People pleasers never are
Extroverts never shut up
Planners never surprise

I think I will go have a cookie

~ Life ~

"Every day, before getting out of bed
I ask 'where is the greatest adventure today?'
I move towards where that is."

Prose

and ribbons and bridges

Coffee Date

So today I had coffee with a former neighbour.

Not that unusual right? Coffee and friends go hand in hand.

Right?

Well, the thing is that this particular neighbour kinda left the neighbourhood in a huff. Was it directed at me? Maybe a little. Maybe a lot. I can't say as I didn't ask. It had been maybe 2 years since we spoke at all and going on 4 years since we had a friendly chat to shoot the breeze.

One thing and another; you know how life moves us forward. Red light, green light - go, go, GO!

Turns out he had some winter tires in his basement that were taking up space he needed. Those tires happened to fit my car. We talked briefly on the phone and he dropped the tires off one day when I wasn't home. The tires and wheels were perfect; he always takes care of his things. One thing and another happened in my life so I didn't get the winter tires on my car when everyone else was doing their annual switch over.

He noticed. Bless him, he's like that. He finally reached out and asked if I needed help putting them on. I said I was waiting for the proper lug nuts to be shipped that were required for the job. The ones I had weren't gonna work; not the right fit.

~ Prose ~

Got the parts a few days later and started to put the tires on this day -- in the middle of a mild snow storm I might add ;-). I invited him over to chat and see how they looked. He countered with come over to the new house and have a beer when I was finished.

Oh, did I mention his young son died a few months back? Yeah, heart breaking.

Not from what you might think -- it was one of those random acts of life that call angels home. No warning, just one morning this beautiful and otherwise healthy young man didn't wake up.

Where was I? Oh yeah. So I go over to his house at the appointed time. I am shown his son's pictures, I am shown his wonderfully written obituary. I see the beautiful new home that the former neighbour and his wife created together. I see the craftsmanship and detail in the building. I see how spotless and clean it is -- so much pride in having the house of their dreams. There's a Christmas tree lit and Christmas music playing.

What isn't there is a loved one who should be there. By all rights he should be there. Hell, he was half my age. Far too young. But that wasn't for me to decide. Nor for the father, nor for the mother to decide.

Maybe you have strong beliefs about what is going on in the world. Maybe you don't really have an opinion. Not for me to tell you what is right and what is wrong.

What I do know is that this one family wishes they hadn't put off a surprise visit, or one more phone call. One family that would give anything to have a do-over with a loved one.

Maybe you are spending this holiday only with certain people, the ones you haven't unfriended on social media. The one's whose opinion matches up with your own world view. Maybe you dis-invited some family members from a holiday celebration. Maybe you were the one dis-invited, for whatever reason.

To me, It's not about right or wrong. It's not about temper tantrums or punishment. It's not about holier-than-thou attitudes. It's about being a human being with love in their heart and a knowing in their souls that together we are stronger. So if you can celebrate this holiday season with 2 or 3 or 4 or 5 or 10 or 50 or 500 or 5,000,000 of your closest and dearest and hopelessly flawed fellow human beings, please do so.

Connections are all when life is short.

~ Prose ~

"I don't know what it will take to get us out of this mess,
but I bet it involves loving outrageously."

Crumble

My inner masculine crumbled last night.

For many, many, many, many years he had placed my inner feminine in a jail cell. The reasons are varied, the reasons are many.

Last night, he realized she wasn't the problem -- he was. He had trampled a rose, he had squashed a ladybug, he had plucked a sunflower whom he felt could not match his majesty.

So he turned the key in the lock on the cage that had been her home. "Click" was all that was heard as she looked into his eyes and searched his soul.

Confidently, quietly, she stepped out of her cell. She glided forward and started to dance. She snapped her fingers, she tapped her toes. She twirled and spun. With a tear in his eye, he remembered her as she was long ago.

He started to speak with a voice that was dry and a throat that was cracked. He coughed in dismay and shame.

With a voice clear and bright, she said "It was not I who was in a cage all those years, for I had my fairies and tea by moonlight."

She had his attention, so she continued more gently "Though I was surrounded by bars, my dear, don't you see? It was

~ Prose ~

you who were caged in a prison without walls, for you were alone in your head, no dance partner in your heart."

As he started to tremble and bend to his knees, she said softly "That is the past, you have learned we are equals.

"Come, let us sup like we did long ago."

the suitcase of mine

so I find myself in a bit of emotional turmoil ... again. that is what happens when you start to heal up the bits that are tender and raw. a bit of healing followed by a bit of turmoil followed by healing, at least in my experience. your experience might be different, yeah?

what activated me this time was making a decision to 'move along' a broken suitcase. it was time. i had meant to move it along a few years back but the old line of "waste not, want not" kept ringing in my ear. so I kept it and used it because it was there in my closet. next to the skeletons apparently. then i would take it on a vacation, and its wheels would wobble, reminding me why i wanted to trash it.

anyway, it was time to toss it out and the opportunity presented itself in the form of an available dumpster. i jumped at the opportunity, as i had a spare suitcase in the attic. the stored one was mom's that she had used for several years, before it became the one-she-wanted-to-chuck. turns out, it was the same make, model and colour of my own suitcase but without the wobbly wheels. ha!

so i empty my suitcase and gather the things to transfer over to the barely used and in great shape "suitcase de attic". mission accomplished ... and then i flip the suitcase over. mom had been fond of purple ribbons tied to the handle of the suitcase to identify it in a crowded airport. mom is in heaven now and some emotions gently bubbled to the surface as the ribbons came into view.

~ Prose ~

but what to do about the ribbons? what indeed. keep them as a token of affection and remembrance of the lady or move those along too? hmmmmm. heartbeat, heartbeat, wipe tear, heartbeat. look up at the ceiling, look back at the ribbons.

i heard a voice in my head. "i have to make the suitcase my own. it's mine now. what do i want on it? choose."

i chose a game of rock-paper-scissors and cut off the ribbons that-were-not-my-style. i chose me, with the addition of a great suitcase that i can have many adventures with. i would like that, and mom would too. as a remembrance -- for a little while anyway.

this new-to-me suitcase, this house, this heartbreak, this day, this life, they are all mine. i can keep what works for me and examine the rest in a dispassionate light. but i have to make them mine. whether that is cutting off ribbons, or switching churches or just making mild changes to things and ways of being that were instilled in me years upon years ago.

i have to make them mine.

Message Overlay In 2023

As my feet touched the floor this morning, the first morning of 2023, I had a song in my head about about the magnetism of love -- you can't get it wrong when it is so right.

I did a tarot card pull for the year ahead for the general population. Now, the cards could be read really "darkly" or they could be read really "light and love filled". Duality universe at it's best. What I loved about the reading is that there was a modifier card as well, that speaks of flowing around obstacles. While I never did record this reading for the socials, it has given me the impetus to start looking at 2023 as a year of working around things - of flowing. It is not a destination year, nor do I feel it is a foundational year -- it is a year of movement. Though whether that is external or internal or a combination is up to each individual.

As prime examples, the washing machine, and the dishwasher are making noise at this moment that is frankly distracting ... or rather the noise would be distracting me if I allowed it to. Speaking of distractions, what is super interesting is that as I type this note of prose out in a rather small computer text zone, there is an even smaller computer message box overlayed upon all of that with a defacto message of "you asked for a function to occur, please wait for it to finish."

The thing is, the computer update function I initiated is stuck in a loop -- it is hung up and won't complete unless I start masterfully pushing buttons. Or I could ignore it. Ignoring it worked by the way, as I have now typed such a wall of text in the text zone, by way of a stylized game of technical

~ Prose ~

peek-a-boo, that the warning message has been shoved out of the way of my active typing -- the @#*& warning box alert is still spinning mind you, but it is not actively impeding my progress. I flowed around it by concentrating on the task at hand. *edit: lesson well learned, I saved (!) my work in another place and reset the computer thus ending the endless loop.

I am calling 2023 the year of adjustment and flow. With a steady heart, one can have the soft boundary of knowning their course. Much like a river that passes around a boulder, the river's action soon turns the large rock to a very smooth pebble. The past three years in particular have moved boulders far more than you might have vision to see at this time. What is your course? Are you flowing to the Sea? To God? To Source? To The All?

Everything can be worked around -- believe it and it so!

Reminded Today

I was reminded today of how easy love can bloom and how easy it is to be stuck in the "poor me, I'm never picked."

The last few days I experienced weird energy ... not exactly lethargic, not exactly depressed, not exactly in the center of my beingness. A feeling of the was-worm as it is almost time to break out of the chrysalis that has changed it, protected it, and allowed it to become ... something new. Or it will, in a few short hours anyway. Anticipation of something but the human is not sure what that will look like.

My days have been stagnant lately. Movement for sure, but not in the way that most humans understand it. Sitting, resting, wondering and feeling a shifting in the upper reaches of the ethers. A subtle growth of the roots that support and stabilize. And I was thinking of her-that-was. The not-so-one-and-only, except she was the-one-that-could break through this stubborn heart of mine by just glowing from her own state of knowing and stability. Did she have it all together? No. Did I back then? No. Do I now know all-I-need-to-know? Not even close. But there was something magical in our connection in a way that no one has come close to replicating. Nor have I found a smile that could melt me in quite the same way.

Or maybe it was me allowing it. Maybe it was "me" that somehow slipped into a crack of my id, or ego, or stories of being un-love-able.

~ Prose ~

So there I am in my chrysalis, just hanging out and mulling my navel. Because really, what the heck else is there to do in a tight cocoon of ooze? Feeling anticipation but also feeling numb in a strange, detached kind of way.

And then today I was guided to walk into a cafe, one of my favourites. Smokin' busy even for a long weekend, even for this popular watering hole. You know the universe is sending big help when you get rockstar parking right in front of a joint when the streets are plugged with cars. I walk in expecting to just order and grab a seat, because you know, that is the usual way...

And there she was. No, not she-of-the-only-one tribe, but she of the hmmmm-that's-a-possibility tribe. Got in line behind her and she immediately started a conversation about how busy it was here. My heart fluttered a little, but I played it cool and engaged in the moment. It was just beautiful to be engaged again in a little convo with a woman that ... had a beautiful smile. Nothing to do but enjoy the moment and practice my confidence ... Except I didn't need to practice. It just was a natural and smooth interaction about a shared experience of waiting.

A wait that was unexpected, shared with a woman that was unexpected.

I love life.

Safety

A winter storm is hitting the area hard. Hard for around here anyway -- the little frozen ice snotballs of snow flakes are slippery around these parts.

The snow plows are out as I find the snow shovel at the back of the garage of where I was welcomed to spend the holidays. Some cobwebs around the handle and dust on the blade but it's good to go. The plan is to shovel the walkway then have a mug of coffee and warm up my hands before tackling the backyard patio. I'm warm. I'm safe. I don't need to travel. When I am done, I can go for a walk in the neighbourhood and see the coloured lights adding a festive touch to the winter wonderland I find myself a visitor in.

The storm passes; the snow stays. The fridge is full and I have nowhere to go. Mmmmmm, turkey leftovers! I am warm. I am safe. I am secure.

The clock ticks forward, the days move along. The weather breaks and the sun is shining now. It is safe to travel on the well plowed roads and a good day to get up early to beat the city traffic. Pack the toothbrush, and pack the jacket Morgan. Away, it's time to head out for home! My real home, my house, where I am safe and secure.

By rights at 5am on a weekday there should be more vehicles but it's holiday time, so the road is mine. A bit of wind but ok.

The wind gets stronger as I pull in for gas and a coffee at a small town many know. The wind is stronger than the coffee, but I am grateful for the warmth and a few words with the old woman who is closing out her night shift at the convenience store. Before I head out, I zip up my cold weather battle gear and remark how warm it is inside the cafe. She smiles and looks away, knowing she will have to fight her own battle soon enough.

Push on, push on. Through the cross wind and the bitter cold. I have heated seats in my car, so I turn them on again. And again. Why can't they just stay on all the time? That would make me happy then I would be safe and secure for a very long time in my 4 wheel drive.

Sunrise breaks, beautiful on the mountains ahead. Trees in snow tresses look as radiant as a bride on her wedding day. Deep breath in, deep breath out. It's a great day to be alive. I had spent this holiday time with family and friends -- good company, good stories and good wine. Yes, it is a good time to be alive. I snick the car heat up a notch, for now I climb up into the colder mountain air. The seat heater turned off again too. I look down to find the seat heater switch and the wheel is grabbed by a slip of ice.

Heart beat, heart beat. The road settles down but my heart does not. Maybe I can be safe without the butt warmer for awhile.

I move over to the right, gently, gingerly for a car to pass. He is safe, he is secure in his mechanical contraption and he wants to go faster than I.

I pull over for a break at a rest stop and there he is again. He sped to the very same stop I am making now. How quaint the place is, with the snow and icicles and Bavarian design. Oh! It was only his dog that needed to stop, so off goes the car, with the human and his puppy happy to be out of the wind.

On goes my winter battle gear, even the toque. My mandated medical mask is a blessing in this infernal cold wind. Step, step, crunch, crunch. It's not so bad. And look how pretty it is! Everything looks like a postcard!! Step, step, crunch, crunch -- oh, maybe it is a little too cold after all! My legs, what is happening to my legs?

Oh right, blue jeans don't stop the cold very well. Walk faster damn it!! Step, step, step, crunch - almost there. Ah, phew, inside again. Open the zippers, remove the gloves, pocket the fogged up glasses. I am safe and warm in the wayside stop.

Ah!

Do up the zippers, put on the gloves, secure the glasses. Time to move out again! Step, step, step, crunch to my beautiful, warm 4x4!

Start up the engine, flip some buttons and heat - glorious H-E-A-T comes out of the vents! Oh yes I smile, there is a God in heaven.

More beautiful scenery drifts by, alight with the clear sunlight of the frigid mountain air. Would love to stop and stare, but can't, there is no room off the snow piled road. It would not be safe, it would not be secure.

~ Prose ~

Onward, onward! Thoughts come, thoughts go. Beautiful scenery. Hmmm, not much traffic coming towards me, how strange! Ah, a truck comes along, he flashes his lights. I think he means the police have set up a speed trap in the middle of this winter wonderland? "Ok! Thank you buddy, I'll watch my speed for a little while". Another car, and another car flash their lights. Ok. I'm in the middle of slowed traffic now, I can't speed anyway but thanks for the heads up fellow travellers!

The cars ahead go slowly around the curves, which is right. It is a bad spot even in good weather, with blind corners. Then I see it.

The car.

The car that hit the rock face and blew out the airbags. That was safe. That was secure. No one is there, nearby, so the driver must be already warm in a car headed to the wayside. And safety. Yes, that is it, everyone is safe.

Traffic slows more, but all I see as I approach the accident is a damaged car and blown airbags. Heart beat, heart beat. The cars ahead keep going, on their very important way.

Then I see her. The driver. She is awake and ok, still in the seat. What do I do? What do I do? I can't stop, there is someone behind me!! I slowly roll past, my mind in a whirl. What do I do, what do I do? The truck behind me wheels over to her. He had time, he knew what to do! Maybe he has blankets and things that would help her. Yes, that's it! She will be safe. She will be secure.

I round the corner and pick up speed. I flash my lights at a truck with over sized wheels coming much too fast up the hill. He doesn't slow, how strange! He is safe, he is secure in his 4x4. No crash, no boom, as he veers out of sight. They are all safe. All safe in their cars.

Yes that's it. They are all safe. They know what to do. The young girl will get to college, like was her plan!

~ Prose ~

Family Array

I finally got a word wrangle -- Morgan style -- on the energy of what is happening in the larger world as of late 2023.

It is as the energy of a family with some young children. The parents are decent folk -- they want their kids to eat their vegetables, wash behind their ears and be good people. The kids are fundamentally ok too, with distinct personalities of their own.

So this entire family goes shopping one day. The day goes well. However, one of the children starts to act up -- wanting to go to the toy aisle, wanting to go home, kicking her brother, all while the parents simply want to get the children new shoes.

The self-centred child eventually breaks away and runs towards the candy store. No one can find her for a few moments. Her brothers and sisters eventually find her in the candy store and encourage her to stop. She does not. She grabs even more candy and slaps it into her mouth.

Mom and Dad come in.

As they come upon the scene of the crime at the candy store, they find one kid shrugging his shoulders and saying "I tried to stop her". They also find one kid in the center of the chaos, with glazed eyes, a sugar twitch and chocolate goo in her hair. The third child is found outside, chasing butterflies.

We leave the family of this story on the sidewalk, after a $100 bill was laid on the candy store counter to pay for the candy and store damage enjoyed by one. The kids all trying to explain themselves at once. Mom is seen cleaning the naughty kid up as best she can, while raging inside with equal parts love and disappointment, and Dad goes to get the car.

~ Prose ~

Future Important

I was afraid of the future. I was taught it was big and scary and I was at the mercy of forces who would dictate to me the path I would follow. "Work hard, and stock pile up!! For the winter will be long and cold and you want to eat and have a warm fire don't you? Day dreams!? Goodness child ... here's a shovel and no more talk of crazy wild adventures! Off with you now, time for gruelling work under the hot sun."

I'm told to be afraid of medical conditions. I'm told that war is necessary. I am told that AI will enslave us all. I am told that forces are marshalling to keep us in our places.

I have a vision of a powerful heart beating inside my very chest.

"Goodness child ... here ... this pamphlet will explain the Plan. Go line up over there with the others to get your number. Don't step out of line, there will be consequences dire!"

Except I have seen the future. It is beautiful and green with much fresh air and love for All. There are no medical emergencies, no wars between nations, or between the genders. No AI to surveil our moves. No forces marshalling, not in this here Future. I will not follow the others. No. I will not.

I will follow Love.

Here To There

I was walking a path from
                        Here to There
Enjoying the day
Smelling the flowers

A little bridge was over a little creek
I stood and enjoyed the burble
and the kurble of the busy little thing

There was the rustle of the leaves
and the bustle of the birds and
                        dragonflies hunting

I breathed in
I breathed out
I gave thanks for my life
and I spit into the water
                        from on high

The droplet hit with much adieu
Its ripple strong

The ripple moved into the creek
into the path of other ripples
                        It faded

I spat again

The ripple of love spread yet again
and meddled with the smaller ripples

~ Prose ~

The creek still flowed

"My ripple was in vain!" I cried out
for the creek had not changed
not one bit
it still flowed along

"No dear one, you did not alter
the flow of water vast
over the pebbles
or around the mud."

"What you did was combine your water with
the water of the creek.
That was enough."

"The path of joy will lead you to the garden of love."

Went

Went speed-dating last night. Really only knew about it from a couple of TV shows. Looked ok, but a little too "movie of the week" for me to ever try....filters of perception be damned. I filed it away for later reference.

Then it became later.

I had seen an early advertisement for the dating event. My brain said "nah". My heart said "maybe." Closer to the event, I saw another advertisement. My brain said "nah." My heart said "maybe baby" and I kept the contact info this time. Signed up the day before the event, cause I am stubborn like that.

My darn heart has been hurt before, why go through all the bullshit again?? Hearts, or my heart anyway, they get battered. They get bruised. They get obliterated in brokenness that takes forever to heal. The messed up thing is they keep coming back for more, like a 2 year old that falls down and goes "ooof" then gets up and keeps on truckin' to whatever very important thing they had in mind.

The day of the event, I woke up and prayed for a peaceful, quiet day. Peaceful morning coffee, an hour at the gym, nice lunch, tea and cookie while I got some reading in, then get ready to go out for the evening. That was the plan. Then the phone rang, the handyman could come and fix the thing. Then the gardeners showed up. Then the neighbour had a loud talk with another neighbour. Then her gardener started up a gas powered leaf blower.

~ Prose ~

Not a quiet day! Didn't they get that the memo this was to be a quiet day in the neighbourhood?

After grinding my teeth a few times, I started to see the blessings in all of this. Got some of my own honey-do-list items crossed off. Had a nice chat with the loud neighbour. Got some of my weeds pulled. Had a cup of tea after the noise died down and realized I had handled it. Yes, it wasn't according to my plan for the day, but I handled it. Activities were beneficial to me, if a little grating on the nerves for a moment or 60. I handled it and I still had plenty of time to fret about the evening ahead!

Oh, no, the evening ahead! What to wear, what to talk about, what to say, what to do?? Arrrrgh! Frickin' heart signing me up for this endeavour. I liked it better when my heart was battered and beaten and shut away in a dark room by itself, eating worms, not able to dictate my life. No, I really didn't enjoy that time of my life -- it is just something I say. I remember the bitterness, the loneliness, the shallowness, the hollowness -- the -ness in general of that period of my life. My head and my heart had agreed several years ago that It was time for another period in my life -- one with beautiful moments, soulful living, joyful expression -- fullness in general and happiness in particular.

My mind raced as I got ready, and it didn't really calm down until I got to the event. There were 4 or more entrances to the large building the event would be held in but it turned out that there was only one door that was open at all.

A large group of us who arrived at the same time, went first to one of the locked doors. I knew right away that they were just like me -- a little nervous, a little lost, but determined to move forward in life. We could handle this set back. The group splintered into smaller pairings to search for the elusive, and rumoured, open main door. I watched them depart, betting with myself on which group might stumble upon success first. I saw the group that found the open door and went to tell the others who had only found other locked doors.

I am not going to tell you it was a life changing evening. I am not going to tell you I found love. I am not going to tell you I found friendship. I am not going to tell you it was a neutral experience.

I will tell you I handled it.

And so did everyone else.

Whispers of the Deep

Here At The Rocks

I'm listening to the surf
listening to the wind
Witnessing the play of the moveable
and the staunchness of the immoveable

I ponder who
could have created such a wonderful play
My soul gets weepy
my soul gets sad
for the longing inside of a time long ago

The tears they come
unbidden it seems
I want to stay
I want to play
here on the Rocks
where my soul is refreshed

Then I hear a calling
it's me calling me
"this is a rest, this a pause"
"nothing here is permanent,
not that rock,
not that bird,
not that tree,
certainly not this human you are"

My journey it seems is not over quite yet
to alleys, to Broadway, to cages,
to jungles and wide open ranges

~ Ciao Bella ~

This journey is mine
and it is not done
The pause is over
and my broken is undone

Ciao Bella

"The revolution does not have to be bloody.
It can be as beautiful as your heart is."

Afterword

Whoa! The world is very different from when I first started writing my poems and prose back in 2018. No doubt you will have your own stories, your own heartbreaks, your own success stories and your own path forward into the Wild Unknown. That is life here on Planet Earth as we gingerly traipse along, headed in the general direction of the third decade of the tumultuous 21st century.

The #wordart I gleefully share here in the Flotsam and Jetsam series came about for the simple fact I met a remarkable woman ... and I lost a remarkable woman ... and then I met other women.

I can tell you that meeting that remarkable woman changed my life. I can tell you the genesis of these poems and ponderings started with her inspiring me. Somehow that inspiration sparked a passion for producing #wordart that continues to this day. Somehow in the mix of our relationship, I became gentler and heart led. Somehow the words I write still have echoes and whispers of that sweet, gentle love, though I know not how.

Will that love return or will there be another? I know that not.

I trust in love and I trust in adventure. If there is more for me of either in this life, I will surely write about it. I know that so.

Morgan Silas Donnelly
January 2025

Also by Morgan

The Flotsam and Jetsam series

Echoes of the Deep
Enchanted Beginnings of Love, Renewal, and Awakening

Whispers of the Deep
Bittersweet Renewal in a Love Lost and a Love Found

Children's Genre

Sammy the Gnat Gets a New Raincoat
If It's Sunny Out, Why Do I Need One?

Meet Morgan

Morgan Silas Donnelly is a poet, writer, speaker and sage whose projects have been called "enchanted whimsy". Themes of self-awareness, unity, and love come into play as he works crafting #wordart. His books Echoes of the Deep, Whispers of the Deep, and Sammy the Gnat Gets a New Raincoat provide perspectives on love and life to different ages and stages.

Visit him online at morgansilasdonnelly.com or follow along on Instagram / Facebook at @morganthewordsmith

Morgan resides and explores in the Pacific Northwest.

This is a sneak peek at my next project.

"The Shipwreck" is from the first book in the "The Tales of the People."

The Shipwreck

I have dropped into the water. It is cold. I am not supposed to be in the water. I am concerned. My ears are ringing, my vision is wonky and I am confused about what is happening.

I thrash around, completely covered by bubbles and cold water spray. I am a little scared. This is not normal. I am holding my breath. I breach the water after a moment and begin treading water.

I hear screams and yelling through my water logged ears. I see a broken ship in the distance. I feel the waves slapping my head. I see a wood plank close by, so I swim towards it. At least now I can float. Where is my family? Where are my friends? Where are the people who were just at the dinner table? Where is the captain?

Oh no, I can see dead bodies. I can see dead bodies that are floating.

There is a storm approaching. There is lightning in the distance. It may rain at any moment. I don't know what happened earlier, but I am scared and alone and there is no one around. I have the board though and I hang on for dear life. I am ok at the moment. I close my eyes to clear the tears, then look down at my body. I am wearing a sailor suit. It had been very starched, it had been very white. Maybe I am part of the crew of the ship that is broken?

Where are my buddies? Are they ok? I look around and I see someone in the distance. I swim towards him. He has no hat on. He always has a hat on. He is spitting water and he is not doing well. He is talking about a wound on his leg. I go towards him as best I can, the waves slapping me making progress difficult. I get to him and I offer him an edge of the board. It sinks a little bit. Just a little bit. I don't think we could have another man sharing the board, weighing it down.

I look around and spot a dark haired man. I call him over. He grabs onto the plank and it sinks even more with his weight. He seems to have a wound on his back of some sort. He is complaining about his back anyway. It is a little hard to hear him above all the other noise now. I realize I am doing better than my friends. I am not injured. I am just dazed.

I let go of the board. It rises up just a little bit. The two of them are ok to hang on, and I can tread water for a bit. There is more debris in view. There is more wood. There are more planks. There are more survivors. Thank God.

Oh, there is a dead body. He is face down. I don't want to see who it is. I might know him.

There are buckets in the debris. Pillows, bedding, things that can float.

Where is help? There must be help! The ship is burning, so there is light for help to see us. Where is help?

More of the survivors gather nearby. The waves are not quite as wild as they were a moment ago. We can see each other and we call out. We know to dog paddle towards each other.

The Shipwreck

I see a life boat in the distance. The group in the life boat is picking up people. There is another life boat even further away, so some of us will make it.

Where is help? There should be help.

Lightning flashes in the distance. Then I see a ship.

My heart goes dark. It is the enemy's ship. It is the one that sank us.

They are moving away. They will not finish what they started. I suppose they think we are just not worth looking for.

I look around and maybe half the people that I know survived. They are getting up on to the life boats. The boats are over crowded already and we are very far out. Me, the buddy, and the other buddy and the little plank. They haven't noticed us quite yet. I try to help the other men by telling them to be strong, be positive and hang on to the plank. One talks about his wife and his kids. The other tells him to shut up, for he is single still but I know there is a girl he is fond of -- a girl he writes to. He hadn't had a chance to let her know how he felt. How he really felt about her. You ever seen a grown man cry? Well .... yeah....

One of the life boats finally does see us. They paddle our way with their oars but they are full up. There is no room. We hang onto the side, others unto some rope. Someone volunteers to give up his seat for the wounded man beside me now. We struggle to get him in the boat, but now he has a seat. He can rest. He don't move too well.

There are more bodies. More debris.

I hang onto the side. I hear the men talk amongst themselves. Someone is freaking out and someone tries to console him. The life boats have come mostly together. That's what you do when there is tragedy. You move together. Companionship. Someone curses and throws his wet cigarettes overboard in disgust. They are wet and they ain't gonna light.

The other ship has moved off, nowhere in sight. Off for another kill.

The storm holds off for now. There is someone in charge. Someone who knows. He says they will come looking for us, our friends. They know where we are, more or less. The battle fleet will come looking.

I ask him "how long?"

He blusters and says "not long."

I don't take the hint and ask him again "how long?"

"Three days. Three days at maximum speed."

Oh uh. Three days. The men fall into despair and go quiet. It starts to rain. The rain comes down as the heavens open up. Misery upon misery.

Dawn breaks and there is no land in sight. The ship has sunk and her debris is scattered. We get our bearings and slowly row towards where we think help might come from. We row half-heartedly. There is no water, no food. Someone has

The Shipwreck

a soggy chocolate bar. He shares it, but it is not enough. The life boats have some food in cans that tastes like shoe leather. It is food though, something to share, something to talk about.

Day fades into dark. We huddle to keep warm. We take turns being overboard, those who can, those who will. It is not strange to hug another man for warmth when you are freezing cold and hungry.

My best buddy is in the next life boat. I know he is alive. It is good to have confirmation.

Night turns into day, and day turns into night. Things are bleak -- men have died in the boats, so we throw them overboard. To make room for the living. Feels very strange to do that.

Day comes, bright as can be. Stomachs are empty and throats are parched. Pants are soiled. Another man dies and I hear groaning.

Then someone says "smoke on the horizon. They have found us! There is hope!"

Those who can, look to see. Yes, there is smoke. Could be a ship! Could even be several ships but are they friend or foe? Do we care?

Someone gets overly excited and stands up, rocking the life boat. He gets hauled down. Don't rock the boat. Be steady and calm. Hold on. The day goes on, and the smoke comes closer. Stan, with his eagle eyes, says yes, it is our friends. The men get happier. There is joy. There is hope.

The ship comes closer and closer. Even the men with vacant eyes start to rejoice and wave. Some of the men jump in the water, and swim towards the ship. Seems strange they would do when the ship is far away.

The ship comes along side, having seen us. It is a ours. Our friends. The ship is small though, almost too small but then we are a small group. The men on board jump down, giving ropes and ladders, and help to those who are struggling. We do our best to take care of the injured and get them up to safety.

It is a hospital ship! Except it is already full to the rafters but there is help for our injured. It is not our battlegroup. The ship is on a mission, a mission to go home. Home. Home sounds nice.

There is no room for our life boats. We cast them adrift. We are all safe and sound, on a hospital ship.

www.ingramcontent.com/pod-product-compliance
Lightning Source LLC
Chambersburg PA
CBHW072158070526
44585CB00015B/1196